BIGGER, BRIGHTER, BETTER

**The story of Bletchley 1944 - 1966
told by its residents**

Edited by Marion Hill

C000003715

Right: The back garden of a house in Buckingham Road, looking towards the brickworks and St. John's Road, early 1960s

Far right: The 1944 Bletchley Co-operative Pageant, performed by local societies to celebrate the centenary of the Co-operative Movement; it was produced by a London Headteacher evacuee and was the start of the 'Bletchco Players'. Syd Maycock, left, is George Washington.

Right: Outside Wilton Hall, waiting for Adam Faith, 1962.

BIGGER, BRIGHTER, BETTER

First published 1996 by Living Archive Press,
The Old Bath House, 205 Stratford Road, Wolverton,
Milton Keynes MK12 5RL (01908) 322568.
Designed by *Dylan* (01908) 200912.
Printed by Amadeus Press Ltd., Huddersfield,
West Yorkshire HD2 1YJ.

Introduction

'Spring will be a little late this year,' sang Deanna Durbin in the hit film of 1944, 'Christmas Holiday'. It was a difficult year for many people on the Home Front : civilian casualties of the War stood at the highest it had been since the Blitz (9,329); income tax took 50% of taxable earnings; and evacuees still vacated London to add greater heartache to those they left, and greater headaches to those they joined (the population of Buckinghamshire alone had been swollen by 35%).

However, 1944 also saw the arrival of the new Town and Country Planning Act which gave local authorities greater powers to acquire land needed for development. By 1966, Bletchley had grown from a small, quiet, country town to a bustling new home for thousands of newcomers, and was destined to become part of the future new city of Milton Keynes.

The 'bigger' Bletchley of 1966 enjoyed, with the rest of the nation, some 'brighter' prospects, too : after the long blackout of the War - only just beginning to be eased in 1944 - the world of the 'Swinging Sixties' seemed a more vibrant place with mini-skirts and the Beatles; with three television channels to choose from (the war years had closed down BBC TV); and with exciting new fashion talents like Mary Quant being 'with it' and receiving an OBE. This strange - and for some, threatening - new 'permissive' society had dawned. Perhaps they might have looked back fondly to the time they danced to the Squadronaires and Geraldo; to when real songs like 'We'll gather lilacs' or 'Lilli Marlene' were sung by the likes of Vera Lynn and Anne Shelton; to when you could go to a special 'ENSA' symphony concert for war workers for a shilling (5p), or see the great Glen Miller in action at Bedford.

Whether what replaced it all was 'better' is the subject of this book. The people of Bletchley tell the story : read and enjoy!

Marion Hill

Castle Estate children on a see-saw, 1962.

Parents, friends and pupils listening to the Headteacher's report during the Wilton School Speech day, 1960.

Bletchley Railway Station, showing Railway Terrace in the background, circa 1950s.

'Just in time for Whitsun!' (Bletchley and District Gazette, 23.5.64). The Queen's Pool opening for the summer with 1,574 'dips' recorded for the three-day holiday, with most of the activity in the new learners' pool, shown here.

1944 Top Hits

'I'm Going To Build A Future World (Around You)'
'When The New World Is Dawning'
'Don't Fence Me In!'

Rickley School Juniors have their Sports Day, 1961, with new houses being constructed around them.

[1] The Vision of the Planners...

I think it's fair to say that the beginning of the thoughts of Bletchley people towards expansion began with the *Gazette's* motto of 'Bigger, Brighter, Better' - we stressed that time and time again. Bletchley was a small town lacking all the facilities that would automatically come with a bigger Bletchley. If the additional facilities - cultural and educational - came with a bigger Bletchley, they would inevitably lead to a brighter and a better Bletchley. The cry for a 'Bigger, Brighter, Better Bletchley' was welcomed by people of all ages - it became the accepted phrase people would use - I am sure it was used in Council. Then, to our great excitement, the Abercrombie Report came out in the middle of the war, naming Bletchley as the suggested site for a new town. The *Gazette* really splashed it!

Ron Staniford

There was something vibrant about Bletchley, even in those days, I think largely due to Bletchley Park - the place buzzed...a busy place.

John Smithie

Bletchley, in ten years, will be a town of 60,000 people, says the Greater London Plan...

(Bletchley District Gazette 16.12.44)

Bletchley wanted to be more than a railway town; it wanted to be a little city.

Bruce Hardwick

There was lack of Government support for the Abercrombie Report, because of Bletchley's problems of sewage disposal and water supply. However, the Council were determined to go ahead with their own plans to improve the town. Water Eaton and the Trees estate were the first to be built; and after the war, with the passing of the Town Development Act in 1952, the Council negotiated back-dated financial support from the Ministry...

Bletchley Council's 5-year plan to expand the town by 5,000, building 1,500 houses at a cost of £3 ½ million was revealed at Tuesday's Urban Council meeting. 'We shall be taking part in one of the greatest social experiments of our time, and thereby improving the lot of thousands of Londoners, whilst at the same time building up the structure of our town to a size that can provide many additional amenities our townsfolk have sought.'

(Gazette 12.1.52)

We spent lashings of money, with the Council sitting through till 2 in the morning - cor, we did work! We were just 12 Councillors, a Town Clerk and a Surveyor (Smithie) with not even a full-time Medical Officer, with a skeleton staff. We started the development of Bletchley. I'm very proud of that.

Ron Staniford

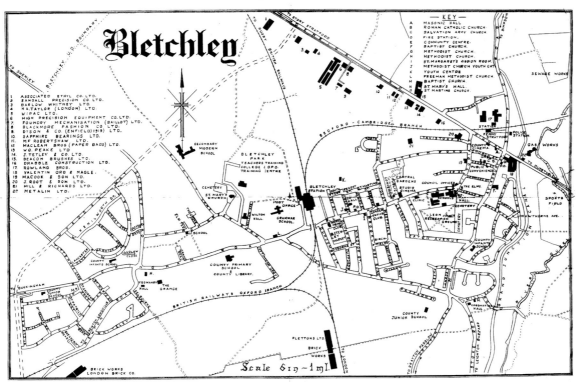

Map of Bletchley Town Centre from the Bletchley Diamond Jubilee Civic Exhibition Guide, 1955.

There was nothing in the Town Development Act for the amenity side; we had many arguments in the London office - Dame Evelyn Sharp, Permanent Secretary, acted like God. She gave me a lecture on how the Civil Service worked; I told her to push for money for amenities.

John Smithie

John Smithie was quite a man. He had tremendous vision... He wanted to get things done and got them done.

Bruce Hardwick

We doubled, trebled, then quadrupled the population to 40,000. It was a huge undertaking for a small authority. We promised not to put one penny on the rates for development - it was difficult, but we honoured it to the end.

John Smithie

Top: John Smithie, Bletchley Town Surveyor, awarded the OBE in 1964 for his work for town expansion.

Bottom: Cllr. E. R. Staniford 'switching in' Bletchley's new automatic telephone exchange in 1957 with his mother, Mrs. A. E. Staniford, and Mrs. J. R. Elmer, who were the original 'hello girls' in 1905.

John Smithie was just a Surveyor from a small urban district in Lancashire. To choose him, we must have been inspired. He went to the top - very temperamental, but all brilliant people are, aren't they?

Ron Staniford

The Vision Takes Shape...

We were proud of getting Bletchley a properly purified water supply, and of the fact that we were able to shape Bletchley into something reasonable. It's the best part of the city to live in, with the South West as the prevailing wind - it blows all the muck away, especially from the brickworks.

John Smithie

BLETCHLEY'S FIRST COUNCIL-BUILT FACTORY OPENED
To Bletchley's ideal road, rail and canal communications, Sir Frank Markham MP on Saturday suggested another attraction for industrialists: the town is 'smog free'

(Gazette 12.12.53)

Amid excitement and rejoicing, Bletchley's own new bright blue plastic swimming pool was opened on Saturday by Miss D. Cohen, Principal of Bletchley Park College. Calling it a minor miracle, she said that ever since the war, those responsible for Bletchley had been working desperately hard on essentials, putting up houses, putting in drainage and putting out clean water. 'But today we have got our little bit of fun. Bletchley's first frolic.'

(Gazette 14.6.58)

Opening the handsome new General Post Office in Bletchley Road, the Assistant Postmaster General, Miss Mervyn Pike, said that although Bletchley's population had increased two-fold since 1935, its postal business had increased three-fold. 'By 1965, not only will we have one of the most modern and up-to-date post offices, but equally will have the most modern and up-to-date telephone system - Subscribers' Trunk Dialling.'

(Gazette 1961)

The Gazette's caption reads : 'Just what we've been waiting for! A joyous crowd climbs the bubbling cascade on the occasion of the opening of the town's own properly - equipped swimming pool.' (14.6.58)

Below: The new head Post Office which opened in 1961.

The Supporters...

Paying tribute to Bletchley, for its help in the over-spill problem of London, Mr. W. F. Deedes, MP, Parliamentary Secretary to the Ministry of Housing and Local Government, said on Wednesday : 'Others may have been first, but certainly no-one has done it better. This can be regarded as one of the pilot schemes in this field.'

(Gazette 12.2.55)

'Half a century hence, the people of Bletchley will be saying how wise their forebears in the 1950s were to take the decision to expand the Town.' Mr. Henry Brooke, Minister of Housing and Local Government, on opening the town's 2000th post-war council house.

(Gazette 17.1.59)

...and the Critics...

Right: Lord Taylor.

Far right: Lord Taylor, third from right, is pictured during his visit to Bletchley outside Dr. Madison's model clinic. Also in the picture : Robert Maxwell, Labour candidate (first left); Cllr. Jim Cassidy (second from left); Cllr. Charlie Head (first right); and Harold Hudson, Town Clerk (second from right).

'Anyone who knows Bletchley knows that it is a very dreary sort of place. It is a terrible place - whoever has the job of redeveloping Bletchley has got his work cut out. It is a real stinker to do, but...it is just the place to tackle.' Lord Taylor.

(Gazette 18.4.64)

He came, he saw - and was conquered. That was the story of Lord Taylor's eight-hour visit to Bletchley...to make amends. 'Of course you are right to tick me off...I am really sorry I said it. It is obvious to anybody that Bletchley is full of life and vigour' ... He worked hard at his job of really seeing the town and meeting its people. As he left the platform of the 'Any Questions' session which ended the day, he was puffing his cheeks and wiping his brow.

(Gazette 23.5.64)

[II] The 'Settlers'

Top: *Members of the staff and employees of Cigarette Components factory, Bletchley, before setting off on an outing to London - their first social occasion since the factory opened three months ago (October 1960).*

Left: *The Bailey family in the doorway of 7, St. Andrew's Road, Coronation Day, June 1953.*

Centre: *Janet Bodimeade with newly acquired pet Rex in Milton Grove, 1961.*

Right: *'Our first crop of tomatoes!' Carole and Janet Bodimeade, 1961.*

Why did they come?

JOBS READY FOR SKILLED WORKERS: LONDON MEN ARE WAITING TO COME
Latest information on the proposed flow of population from London to Bletchley is that local firms have listed immediate vacancies for more than 20 skilled men...All five exporting authorities, Acton, Willesden, Wembley, Hendon and Harrow, have submitted lists of recommended men who want to come to Bletchley as soon as there is a house and a job available for them.

(Gazette 26.6.52)

You came with the job - you had to have a job - the job went with the house really...Ronnie was on the railway and his wages were about £7 - it was about £3 for the rent, so you didn't have much left. I don't know how we managed. I think we just got deeper and deeper into bloomin' debt...There used to be a shop thing come round, a mobile shop - that was a laugh...he had all these goodies on the van. We used to get x amount of stuff, but we didn't have to pay until the end of the week.

Pat Flinn

Little two-bedroom house, beautiful house...we went back and said 'Yes, we'll accept it, I'll accept the job.' About a week or so later they said we could go and get the key for the house and start work at the Marston Brick Company. We thought it was magic.

Alec Clifford

Alec and Betty Clifford and their sons Alec Jnr. and Gary in the back garden of 19, St. Paul's Road, 1958.

We lived in 2 rooms on the second floor of a house in Islington, 5 flights down to the toilet and as the children were small they weren't allowed to use the toilet because it wasn't very clean and so when we moved to Bletchley they were so pleased that they'd got a toilet they could use, Linda locked herself in the first day we moved in.

Pam Porter

'Oh! it's lovely after what I've been used to,' says Mrs. J. O'Shea of 6, St. Paul's Road, who used to live with her husband and three small children in two upstairs rooms at Harrow. 'We had to carry up our water in buckets and cook on a gas-ring,' she adds.

(Gazette 25.7.53)

Ken, Vera and David Barrow outside their newly acquired house during the Coronation, 1953.

What was the move like?

It was a hot, hot day. A lorry turned up, picked up all the stuff. We came down to Bletchley by train, which seemed to take an awful long time to get here. Getting out at Bletchley Station, it was very rural, and I thought, 'This is great.' There was all hedges all along Station Approach - one side was what had been old wood yards and stabling and it was all picket fence along the station side...We walked along Buckingham Road - all trees along there - up until we got towards Avon Grove, then it became new and stark. The difference was like stepping onto the moon.

Michael Brace

We arranged for a vegetable lorry to bring us down...it rained all the way...we got in and me son's cot mattress was soaking wet - we couldn't put him on that. We lit the gas oven up...

Alec Clifford

I loaded up the night before on my lorry. I was ready to leave at 7. Sylvie saw to the girls and I put the rest of the stuff on the wagon, sheeted it down and that's it. She was an open-backed wagon, couldn't even afford a removal truck. The day we moved in here - which was on a Saturday - by the coming week, we had ten bob each, me and Sylv. That was 1960.

Frank Bodimeade

I can remember coming in the back of a big lorry, waving goodbye to someone - but I can't remember who.

Laura Owen

Above: *The Bodimeade family home in Milton Grove, 1960.*

Left: *Sylv and Frank Bodimeade with Aunt Jess at Woburn on a picnic in 1963.*

First impressions...

BLETCHLEY'S FIRST 'SETTLERS' FROM LONDON ARRIVE

Looking out of the door of their first-ever home, across the churned-up land that will be their garden to the other houses now in every stage of erection, Mr. and Mrs. Atwell thought they were going to like Bletchley very much, were thrilled with their house ('But you can't get into the larder to sweep it out,' added Mrs. Atwell) and full of praise for the local council.

(Gazette 6.9.52)

I moved to Bletchley from Islington with my Mum when I was 3 years old, which would be 1956.... We lived in Whaddon Way...we were the first people to move into the house and my vague recollection is just of a sea of mud...

Wendy Marshall

We felt like gypsies really coming up here, all with our thick, muddy wellingtons...we used to plod on down. About two buses a day. We used to walk everywhere.

Joan Burchell

I remember within the first couple of weeks of coming here, the freedom, you know, going out on your bikes down St. John's Road which ended at the top - there was nothing there...it was like a glorified playground really.

Stephen Flinn

Above: In four weeks, 50,000 tonnes of earth were moved from the rear of Park Street to widen the Oxford-Bletchley branch line near the Newfoundout, October, 1959.

Right: The Counties Estate, pictured in 1961.

The day I arrived, I walked down Buckingham Road to Fenny Stratford. I said to a lady, 'How much further is it to Bletchley?' She said, 'You've just come through it!' It reminded me very much of a Wild West town.

Betty Watts

Where you've got the links golf course...that was a disused RAF camp...there was all open space over on that side, the right side of Buckingham Road. Where Whaddon Way was, it was all open land, and it was a lot quieter. That's what we couldn't get used to at first, the quietness of the place.

Alec Clifford

I used to go shopping and wonder how - all the houses looked alike - and I used to think, "Ooh, where do I live?" It was so peculiar really, 'cause they're dead alike.

Betty Clifford

Above: A mechanical excavator at work on the Bletchley swimming pool site, March, 1958

Left: Whaddon Way, Bletchley

My wife was over the moon, you can't believe it, to get out of the tip where we was living. Course, it was a great disappointment when we got here : when I took and showed her our house, it was a re-let - the older type of house on the Saints estate, St. Paul's Road, compared to what my brother had. It was all right, though... When I moved down here, there's no doubt about it, if I lived in London I don't think me and the wife would have been together now. No, no way. When I was down there, I'll be honest, I was a newly-wed and I was out every night with me brother drinking. It was only my mother-in-law who made me realise that when you're married, you're supposed to live together.

Bobby Bunn

I do remember my Dad saying he felt so grateful being given the opportunity by this country - being given a job, what to English people wouldn't have seemed very much, but because they had nothing, you know, they felt like they were living in the lap of luxury.

Pietro Palmiero

Bobby Bunn's wedding day, September 1955.

'It's just like being a film star,' says Mrs. H. E. Newman, tenant of the thousandth post-war Bletchley council house which was opened by Mr. Harold Macmillan, Minister of Housing and Local Government, last week. 'As soon as I say '35 St. Clement's Drive,' everyone seems to know me...I only hope people won't point me out as 'that London woman,' she laughed.

(Gazette 31.10.53)

When I walked through my own front door, it was just like I'd been given a million pounds... I think it was about a month before they put the fences and that up, and then it was lovely 'cause your garden you started from scratch - that was right up my husband's street, to start his garden from scratch.

Doreen Brace

Top: 'Pop' Barrow digging the garden in St. Andrews Road, 1953.

Below: Pictured outside Bletchley's 2,000th post-war Council house, 18, Kennet Drive, are, left to right, Cllr. W. Caldwell; the Minister of State for Housing and Local Government, Mr. Henry Brooke; Mr. C. Drabble, the builder; the tenants of the house, Mr. and Mrs. B.R.Spencer; and Sir Frank Markham, MP.

It was weird feeling of being someone new in somewhere old, being the first on the block as it were...The key to it all was actually starting to do something, and the something that you do obviously if you're at school age is go to school.

Michael Brace

Bottom: Holne Chase School, 'Class of 1955'. Irene Spanner (née Davies) who supplied this photo is third from right, second row from the back.

Enjoying the new life...

'I do think the Council have everything very well organised...there is every consideration to the tenants who are moving in, a welcome letter, the key of the door just where they said it would be and everything laid on.'

(Mr. H. Rundle, Gazette 15.11.52)

I can remember the house we lived in, in Bletchley : it was new; there was no road; there was open farmland along the right hand side - the cows used to come down there and feed out of a trough.

Barry Brace

When we moved, the street was full of Italians : there were so many people compared to Milton Keynes village. I played with all the Italian children, went to all the weddings. They were absolutely wonderful affairs, in the old Coronation Hall, with 200 plus people. We used to get big pastries full of custard, and almonds in little pieces of net, and the wine - oh! - we were allowed to drink it!

Gisella Perry

Above: *Vera Barrow pegging out washing during her first winter in Bletchley, in a garden with no boundary fencing.*

Right: *The wedding of Miss Maria Foresteiro and Mr. Iwan Prociw (Gazette, August 1962).*

Bletchley Cattle Market circa 1950s. The main picture shows Mr. Wheeler, the stockman on the left, inside the pen.

Beautiful market, Thursday and Saturday. Betty used to go down there on a Thursday, and we're talking about the days when chicken was a luxury, not like it is today. They'd auction the chickens - live chickens - and she'd get one for about 1/9d (9p). It had to be killed before it left - she paid the auctioneer's assistant 3d (1p) to wring its neck, so you had to pluck it and gut it yourself.

Alec Clifford

The cattle market was the one thing the children really enjoyed when they came here - they felt they were in the country. The children used to love to see the calves. To me, it looked a bit cruel, clipping their ears, but then not coming from a farming family, we did not know how to treat them.

(Member of Mothers' Club)

The highlight of the week was Bletchley Market. You'd get the villagers come in, but the bus timetables were so dreadful, they might come in at 11am and had to go back at 11.20! The fashions of some of the village people who came in went back to the 1920s.

Betty Watts

Mum and Dad said Bletchley was a lovely country town. I couldn't imagine what 'an estate' was - we came from a mass of houses. I couldn't imagine a new house in a country setting.

Michael Brace

At the top of Tattenhoe Lane, we just used to pop across and go blackberrying. It's all houses now. And that was lovely, getting blackberries and make a blackberry and apple pie. And the bluebell woods.

Vera Barrow

On a Sunday morning, Dad always used to take me for a walk down Tattenhoe Lane, and sometimes we used to fish for tiddlers, and walk up to the Farmhouse.

Wendy Checkley

Not many people had cars; most people cycled. A most wonderful sight was when people were finishing work at night, Buckingham Road would be absolutely glowing with cycle lamps.

Betty Watts

Top: Derek Brace fishing for tiddlers in the 1960s.

Right: Wendy Checkley (née Brace) blackberrying in Tattenhoe Lane in the late 1950s.

Far right: Bletchley Road in the snow, 1962.

The Shoulder of Mutton used to be where The Three Trees is. We used to go in there. In those days, every pub had a piano and a sing-song. There was one who had a voice like Donald Peers and his name was Jimmy Quinn. You could bet your life if Jimmy Quinn walked in the pub, within a quarter of an hour, everyone in the pub would be singing. We owed our social evenings to Jimmy Quinn, his personality and flair. He was probably 37 then. He used to take off Dickie Valentine.

Bobby Bunn

I took my brother down The Shoulder. I said,' Here's our local pub.' It was just a bar and a cellar. The bloke would take the beer out of the barrels. 'Cor blimey,' he said. 'Funny place this.' It had a thatched roof then, just a room and a cellar where the barrels were.

Ronald Flinn

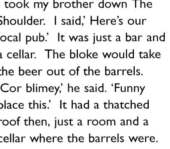

We'd hear old **Bobby Bunn's** van burping up the road...He had a mobile shop - used to sell everything, lucky bags of sweets for the kids and crisps, tea, sugar, potatoes...he used to come up with his old washing machines, half-a-crown an hour he used to charge. We used to push it to one house then another. We used to have a scream! He knew we did it as well. So that half-a-crown done about 4 lots of washing, so he didn't get rich out of the likes of us.

Joan Burchell

Above: The 'Shoulder' circa 1950s.

Centre: The closing of the 'Shoulder' - last orders after 200 years, in 1962.

Below: The 100th broadcast of the BBC's 'Hello Mum' came from the Plough Inn at Simpson. All gathered round the piano singing 'All the nice girls love a sailor' with Harold Brewer at the piano, and Tony Clay on the accordion. (May, 1958).

We'd lose such a lot of weight in sweat...my wrists used to swell up. I had to put all bandages round them. They swelled up with the different movement of your wrists of stacking the bricks. You put bits of inner tubes on your hands - with little slits to put your finger through, so the bricks didn't burn your hands.

Alec Clifford

Although the Saints' estate is so near the eleven tall chimneys of the London Brick Company's works, the air there is credited with being the best in the district, and many ex-London mothers are saying that their children have never been so well in their lives...

(Gazette 25.7.53)

Above: *Boys' race at Newton Road showing the brickworks chimneys in the background, 1953.*

Right: *Bletchley brickworks at sunset, 1962.*

The brick dust used to live with us...They used to say to us that it never affected our health, but on a summer's day you could taste the stuff in the air, the sulphur...it was awful - and all the cars would always be covered in a red sort of dust and if you put your washing out and it rained, you'd have to wash it again because it'd be filthy.

Alan and Wendy Marshall

...*from the WATER :*

OUR BROWN WATER BLUES Bletchley's brown water troubles were stirred up again at Tuesday's Council meeting. The 'obnoxious fluid called fresh water' was almost continuous now, it was alleged, and a source of complaint from housewives though it was known to have no harmful effect on health. The trouble is caused by sediment in the old mains and flushing is being tried as a remedy... 'At our factory (Wipacs) a few days ago, 40 gallons of tea had to be poured away because the workers would not drink it because of the water,' said Coun. D. A. Pacy.

(Gazette 18.4.53)

We used to have to filter the water. I don't know how they got away with it. It was brown - it was terrible.

Iris Witcomb

A GLASS OF CLEAR WATER AT LAST!
Filtration Plant Results Exceed Expectations

(Gazette 29.8.56)

The WIPAC factory in Watling Street circa 1959.

...from the INSECTS :

THE FLY PLAGUE The item of by far the greatest public interest and concern was that of the plague of flies from which Manor Farm estate and parts of Water Eaton, in particular, have been suffering...

Cllr. Mrs. Ramsbotham said that in one or two cases, babies had been put out in their prams and their faces had been smothered with flies; and in another case, a jug of milk had been put down and in a few seconds nine flies had committed suicide in it...

A mother related that on Sunday she had to stand over her children waving a newspaper while they ate their dinner so that the flies could not settle on the food...

As well as proprietary fly-papers, cards and sprays, saucers of treacle and bundles of mint have been some of the suggestions put forward as counter-measures. 'We have killed literally thousands of flies in the past week or two,' said one woman in Pinewood Drive. 'It has really been horrible.'

(Gazette 17.7.54)

An army of red insects resembling minute spiders are invading St. Clement's Drive houses, Bletchley. Residents who are out for most of the day come home to find insects swarming in their hundreds...

One housewife told a reporter that an urban official had issued her with a box of white powder. 'This has not had any effect. They just run around with the powder on their back!'

(Gazette 12.5.56)

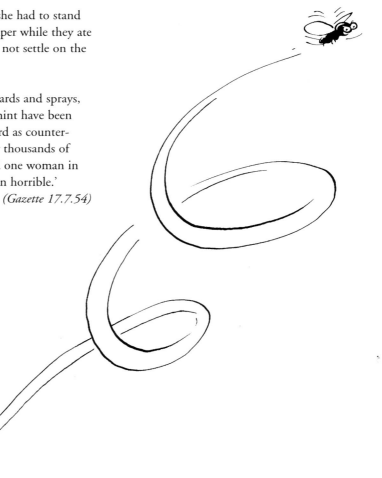

...and from the SEWAGE WORKS!

Bletchley's new sewage works smell - and the Council admits it. Cllr. C. Head said that when he went to bed at night with the windows open for fresh air, what he got was the smell of these sewage works : 'We spend £215,000 and what we are doing at this end of the town is getting stunk out, and properly stunk out'...

Cllr. Mrs. Ramsbotham suggested that as they apparently needed flies to take away the smells and they got so many complaints about flies from their refuse tips, they should put the refuse tips near the sewage farm!

(Gazette 9.7.55)

In the sweltering heat of Wednesday afternoon, I stood in the midst of Bletchley's sewage works sniffing the sweetly-scented air. The previous day, the Council had installed an apparatus which they hoped would kill THAT SMELL *(writes 'Gazette' reporter 6.7.57)* ...Here I was on the pump-house roof where two small guns were spraying scent onto the air from a ten-gallon drum said to last four days without replenishment.

What was it like for the children?

It was a new school - various parts of it weren't completed. There were new people joining all the time. You got certain teachers that were strict : our form teacher used to put about four rulers together and hit you across the knuckles - and that was a female!

Barry Brace

We used to go swimming over the gravel pits, just off the A5. There were always gangs and bullying at school - always has been. They used to call us Londoners, we used to call them 'carrot crunchers'; but after a while it became integrated - you did get friendly with some of them.

Barry Brace

Above: Church Green Road Infants on their first day of School, September, 1963.

Right: Castle Infants schoolchildren watch a rehearsal of 'Alice in Wonderland' in December, 1959.

Far right: John Harvey and Barry Brace lead a group through the water jump in a cross-country run from Wilton Secondary School, March 1958.

LONDON CHILDREN DAMAGE FARMLAND

London children from Bletchley's new estates are damaging local farmland, a Bletchley area farmer declared at a NFU meeting. Complaint was first made by Mr. H. Ramsey of Windmill Hill Farm, Old Bletchley : 'You cannot leave a rick anywhere; they run your sheep and pull your hedges. It is no use farmers speaking to them for they take no notice. They are like a swarm of locusts. We like to see kids enjoying themselves, but not in that way.'

(Gazette 22.5.54)

I remember going over the brickworks, big gangs of us. I can remember an old plane that had come down - must have been a war plane; we used to play in that - camps. There was a great big high bridge with a little girder on it that we used to run along - very dangerous, I know. We used to play 'chicken' with the brick lorries in Newton Road.

Laura Owen

The old haunted house, at the bottom of Majors Hill - it's now The Three Trees, used to be The Shoulder of Mutton. That was all shut down then - we used to go in there and play. Before they did it up, it was all derelict. Also, where the Poets' estate is, Buckingham Road, that was all derelict. There was a big old house in there with a big swimming pool - I remember playing there. Nobody used to bother you ... A load of us used to take off and take sandwiches to this place right up Tattenhoe Lane, I think where the prison is now. There was a little tiny chapel up there, hidden in the woods. We had our little secret places.

Laura Owen

Laura Owen (née Flinn) in Tattenhoe Lane circa 1964.

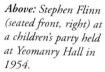

Above: Stephen Flinn (seated front, right) at a children's party held at Yeomanry Hall in 1954.

Top right: Members of Bletchley Road Methodist Sunday School waiting for their transport to a pantomime, January, 1958.

Centre: Water Eaton Juniors at their end-of-term Christmas party, December, 1957.

Bottom: Saints' Junior schoolchildren watching a conjuring act, November, 1957.

[III]   The 'Natives'

Melville Farm, off Shenley Road, circa 1960s.

What was it like for Bletchley people ... in 1944?

Bletchley Road circa 1944.

Crosses of sticky brown paper covered the windows of public buildings; air-raid shelters were erected at convenient points around the town with flat concrete roofs, paling gates and the key hung behind glass outside; static water tanks were erected on waste land adjoining Bletchley Road and bags of sand lay outside private houses; blackout was strictly enforced and air raids were heralded by the siren on the roof of the council offices and accompanied by the howling of every dog in the town.

Ted Legg

...in the nation as a whole,

- *Less than half a million crimes were known to the police (in 1995, there were over 5 million);*
- *Four and a half million people served in the armed forces;*
- *The normal working week was 46-47 hours;*
- *There still was not equal pay for women teachers;*
- *10 million radio licences were issued;*
- *One and a half million people went to the cinema each week;*
- *The new Education Act was passed, bringing in state Grammar Schools;*
- *John Profumo was MP for Kettering;*
- *8 million people belonged to Trade Unions;*
- *There was no dole, and no 'teenagers';*
- *Prisoners of War were helping to rebuild Britain's houses...*

The brickyards during the war had a huge number of Italian prisoners working there. They used to come to lunch on a Sunday - my parents had invited them; so were these women from Bletchley Park who were billeted with us and who were translating the secret messages that these guys had been putting into operation. It was a funny old world.

Barrie Field

The prisoner of war camp was at Drayton Parslow, which then became a GPO training centre.

Barrie Field.

The back garden of 86 Eaton Avenue, looking south towards Larch Grove before any houses - and Manor Road School - were built, circa 1944-5. Later, PoWs helped to build the Trees estate.

...after the war ended?

It gradually altered after the war - there were more shops in Bletchley Road. We called it 'Tin Town': there were little lock-up tin shops. Mrs. Perrin had a cake shop; there was a small sweet shop; Green started off selling second-hand furniture; Elizabeth's Hat Shop was there; then there was Covent Garden's fruit shop, then the goods yard for the railway where the coal was dealt with...

Winifred Ottery

Top: 'Where the road will go' : the changed alignment of Bletchley Road under the new main-line railway bridge in 1960 meant the end of 'Tin Town' (under the bridge).

Right: Syd Maycock, wearing his Council Chairman's regalia in 1946.

Far right: Leonard Grigg in a pushchair in front of Woodbine Terrace circa 1945. There was no back garden, and only about 7 feet square in the front. It was tucked away behind the old County Cinema. The houses were demolished to make way for the new telephone exchange.

My Uncle, as Chairman of the Urban District Council, helped in the expansion. The town grew around me gradually. My family thought the growth was a good thing.

Roy Maycock

People I knew as evacuees are still here, as are some from Bletchley Park. People used to say, you could tell a Bletchley Park person - one red sock, one blue, eccentric, upper middle class, but intelligent.

Roy Maycock

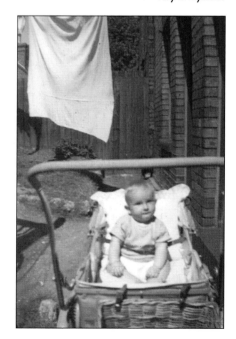

Just after the end of the war, they had German prisoners working on Chestnut Crescent, digging for drains and laying roads for the first new houses. Then they built Larch Grove.

Roland Doggett

The prisoners were very cheerful *(left)*. One or two spoke English. One told us that he was a civil engineer in Germany and was looking forward to the time when he would be going home. None of them seemed bombastic. They all seemed quite happy, and had no objection to being photographed.

(Gazette 15.9.45)

Above: *Mrs. Grigg and baby Leonard by the thatched cottage in Mill Road, Water Eaton, just behind Larch Grove, circa 1950.*

Left: *The first day after sweet rationing ended, outside Jack Pariss' shop in Victoria Road, Bletchley. Also shown : Mr. Bell's Outfitters and Fennemore's Undertakers.*

When Bletchley began to grow ...

There was barely a bus service at first - you walked everywhere.

Bob Berry

At that time the brickworks were going flat out - at Newton Longville they were working day and night, the brickworks at Skew Bridge were going like anything, Captain Mells and his Flettons Brickworks were going like anything. The whole area was really quite prosperous.

Dick Arnold

A lot of people worked at the brickyards - obviously, bricks were big business then because of all the war damage. You saw train after train just full of bricks going all over the country.

Barrie Field.

Above: A rare sighting of a Bletchley bus - this one in 1962.

Top right: Building the Oxford/Cambridge freight line, circa late 1950s.

Right: Trainspotters, 1962-style. David Barrow, pictured as a baby on page 11, is 3rd from right. David Atwell (see page 14) is behind him.

They started to build - the Trees estate - at the end of 1945. The first houses were for those who most needed them. People who had plenty of money were getting Council houses - they couldn't buy, as no private houses were being built. There was a sort of points system - a housing officer would come round. By the time I got one, there were more houses about.

Arthur Grigg

THE NEW TENANT

First tenants of Bletchley's new Council houses are a family of three, father and child both tuberculosis patients who are now completely separated - father in a hotel, child in an open-air school, and mother with her own family. The good news was conveyed to Mr. and Mrs. J. W. Harman yesterday, and they hope to move into the house in a week's time. Mr. Harman considers that the moving into a new house will add years to his life: 'You could not want anything better if you were a millionaire.'

(Gazette 29.6.46)

THREE DAYS IN THE LIFE OF A NEWTON ROAD HOUSE

Bletchley's Trusteel houses are now going up in Newton Road. The Gazette photographer has recorded on successive days this week the story of rapid progress in construction.

(Gazette 17.5.47)

How Bletchley people felt about the growth of the town : the good news...

There were more members of the public present than usual when Councillor Johnson introduced the plan in a very impressive, sound and statesmanlike speech. They listened with rapt attention, and took spare copies of the council's statement and plan home with them.

(Gazette 12.1.52)

The expansion brought more jobs, more shopping, a lot more traffic through Fenny on the Victoria Road : everybody from the Saints Estate had to come through Bletchley, around and back - to get to work along the Denbigh Road ... Bletchley did become 'Bigger, Brighter, Better.' When I came home on leave from Germany in 1953, we had a Woolworth's - it was amazing to see this in Bletchley.

Roland Doggett

Top: *Bletchley Road, with Woolworth's in the centre, circa 1959.*

Above: *The staff of the Bletchley branch of Woolworth's at a dinner at the premises, December, 1959.*

Right: *Aylesbury Street in Fenny Stratford, circa 1959.*

There was a sympathy - a gratitude - that they weren't in London having been bombed out. My memory is of something of an ambivalence : they were quite happy with the old world, but the new world had arrived and changed everything. Everyone was keen to start a new way of going on - the development was all part of that.

Barrie Field

They've never had it so quiet. That is the opinion of people living or working along the Bletchley stretch of the Watling Street following Monday's opening of the M1 Motorway. Shoe-repairer, Mr. G. Brown who works just a few yards from the Fenny traffic lights said, "It's marvellous - it's just like a cemetery.."

(Gazette '59)

Above: *The Rivers Estate, circa 1959.*

Left: *Watling Street, looking towards Little Brickhill from the canal bridge at noon two days after the M1 opened, November, 1959.*

: the bad news...

We did hear things like they are only letting the rough people come down, which put our backs up, but once they did come, we realised that wasn't the case. We had a lot of decent people.

Monica Austin

Below: Congestion in Bletchley Road, December, 1960.

Bottom: A view of the Home Farm area in June 1960, taken from the top of St. Mary's Church tower.

Londoners were classed as 'wide boys' and viewed with suspicion - they were a bit fast. There were two totally different ways of life : up there, the big city ; here, you're in the country.

Bob Berry

Often, people used to say, 'Ooh, these Londoners'. I thought it was very sad, wasn't it, 'cause after all they wanted a decent home to live in, didn't they?

Marjorie Clarke

I think everybody thought Londoners were rogues.

Alec Clifford

We knew Bletchley had to increase, what with the evacuees and Bletchley Park - a lot married locally, so we needed more housing. But some locals were upset at losing a lot of walks and open space.

Eileen Corden

The people who were actually born there didn't like people coming in because they said it spoilt all the countryside and it spoilt everything by them coming in.

Doreen Brace

The new Bletchley brought problems for locals
- with HOUSING :

My uncle was Assistant Clerk of Works and he used to have to go round inspecting these places. He used to say they'd got coal in the bath, the doors are missing because they've had them off for burning fuel. He used to be furious over it. He said, 'You bring them down from London, put them in decent places and this is what happens.' It really used to get him cross.

Eileen Corden

A 'HEARTBREAK PROBLEM' : Cllr. W. Caldwell stated that it would be leading local people up the garden path to put them on a housing list when at the present rate of allocations there would be none available for them for nearly four years. Cllr. Mrs. J. Ramsbotham said this was a grave problem - they were delighted to house people from overcrowded areas. But at the same time their own Bletchley people were just stuck on this list.

(Gazette 1955)

- with SHOPS :

St. Mary's Road shops, 1953.

Travelling shops which tour the town and which pay no rates are seriously affecting the business of the highly-rated local shops. Cllr. Head thought they should have the advice of their medical officer on certain aspects. For instance, he understood that paraffin and foodstuffs were being hawked from the same vehicle - which he thought food shops were not allowed to do.

(Gazette 1.3.58)

There was a bit of controversy when my husband and others came out of the army. It was the official opening of the first two houses, and the person who was getting the first one didn't even live here. The men went down and stopped one getting it. It was about a year before we got a house. We had to stay with Mum, then got a house down the road.

Winifred Ottery

There's a famous saying in this town : 'Where do you come from? The other end.' The railway bridge was the dividing line - the London Estates were 'the other end'.

Bob Berry

Above: Freight travelling across the fly-over, 1961.

Right: Twelve-hour shifts were worked by men moving over the Oxford branch line to its new position at the Newfoundout, a switch made necessary by the sweep of the new fly-over, November, 1959.

- with JOBS :

We did feel they were pinching jobs from local people ... when we got engaged, we put our names down for a house (but) you just couldn't get one like that, whereas if you'd come from London, provided you'd got a job here ... you'd move straight into a new house and there was a bit of resentment there.

Roland Doggett

- with CHILDREN :

After some discussion on the urgency of providing space for the children to play, Mr. Staniford said, 'Come with me down to Whiteley Crescent where there is a children's playing space. You will find it practically empty. But you will find dozens of children playing cricket on the flower beds which we try to keep up. It is the same with the Leon recreation ground, one of the biggest grass stretches for miles around.

(Gazette 12.7.58)

Above: The opening of Berry's Electric Company Ltd., 1961. Here, the famous 'Magicoal' fires were assembled.

Left: First day back at school for Bletchley Road Secondary Modern pupils, 1963.

Local Bletchley characters :

Top right: Cllr. Charlie Head with Japanese visitors from Kobe in St. David's Road, 1963.

Centre left: Horace Hardwick receiving the Ramsbotham Cup from James Ramsbotham at the Bletchley August Show at Manor Fields, circa 1950.

Centre right: Norman Green and Roy Young with the magic lantern from Dr. Fegan's Homes, bought in a recent Bletchley market sale, 1961.

Bottom left: Cllr. Mrs. Julia Ramsbotham, Bletchley's first woman Chairman of the Bletchley Urban Council, being invested with the chain of office by Cllr. W. Caldwell, May, 1960.

Bottom right: Harold Hudson being welcomed to office with his wife Elsa by the outgoing Town Clerk, R.L. Sherwood, 1960.

Charlie Head - quite an exceptional man - he could sketch a farm building on the back of an envelope and build it by eye; Norman Green started the stall market on the corner of the cattle market - he was the local bookmaker, the local furniture shop, the local antiques chap; the florist Jimmy Ramsbotham had a lot to do with the development of Bletchley and Fenny - his wife was chairman of the town council for two or three years at the vital time. She was the girl who could get things done.

Dick Arnold

I remember some of the local councillors - they put their heart and soul into it. Bill Caldwell - he never had a car - he used to walk around. The estates were kept wonderful; no cars were allowed on the grass - Smithie would send a letter. I thought the Council were wonderful - they got involved.

Arthur Grigg

New Council Chamber

BLETCHLEY Council met in its new Council Chamber for the first time on Tuesday evening and this special *Gazette* composite photograph by Dan Johnson shows councillors and officials before the start of the business. On the dais, left to right, are Lt.-Col. D. H. Waldron, the area Medical Officer of Health; Mr. J. F. Smithie, the Surveyor and Engineer; Cllr. C. Head, Vice-Chairman; Cllr. Mrs. D. Ramsbotham, Chairman; Mr. H. V. Hudson, Clerk to the Council; and Mr. Norman Chambers, the Council's Treasurer. Office staff include Mr. T. Sheldrick, Mrs. J. Orchard, Mr. T. Holderness and Mr. R. J. Storey. The Press bench is seen at right centre rear.

Councillors round the horse-shoe shaped table, mainly with their backs to the camera are, left to right, Cllrs. E. W. Daniels, W. G. Graver, G. Lumb, M. Tompkins, L. Cowley, H. J. Price, W. Caldwell, F. Evans, J. Cassidy, Miss E. M. Gillett, C. G. O. Clarke and R. Fisher.

Top centre: Bill Caldwell, when he stood as a Labour Councillor for the Eaton Ward in May, 1966.

Top right: 'After the count': Robert Maxwell MP, 'overcoated and scarved because of his cold', is photographed with his wife and son, Phillip, after he won the constituency seat for Labour in 1964.

Above: St. Martin's Church Mothers' Union circa 1952, taken on the corner of Vicarage Road and Aylesbury Street in the gardens of Fenny Stratford Vicarage, now demolished. Eileen Corden is in the back row, second from right. Her daughter, Susan, is on the ground, far right.

Centre left: Elsa Hudson presenting prizes at a children's dancing competition, Water Eaton, 1952.

Bottom left: The new Council Chambers, 1962.

Above: Michael Brace working on a grinding machine at Filtrona in the mid 1960s.

Above right: The BBC's 'Workers' Playtime' broadcast from the W.O.Peake factory in May, 1959 with Bernard Spear (left) and singer Don Lang.

Bottom: Department Managers of the Bletchley Co-op, September, 1952.

Above: At the opening of the new branch library in 1962, four Headmasters, one businessman and a local government officer! From left to right : M.V. Jones (White Spire), D. Halewood (Bletchley Grammar), B. Harding (Holne Chase Juniors), D.B. Bradshaw (Bletchley Road County Secondary), W.S. Johnson (auctioneer and surveyor), N. Chambers (Bletchley UDC Treasurer).

Top left: A welcome for Father Christmas in Bletchley Road, 1961.

Left: Bletchley Town Football Club, 1962.

Ready For The Kick-off

Bletchley Town-United F.C., whose first United Counties match is next Saturday, had their first official trial on Tuesday. Our picture (DJ4993) shows Mr. G. Malster, Vice-Chairman (front) and team-selector Mr. Jack Ansell with players who took part in the game. They are, left to right, standing: B. Fussell, A. Pickersgill, P. Green, K. Stevenson, B. Liscoe, A. Smith, K. Hartwell, D. Lines, T. Clarke, R. May, R. Patten, R. Hale; kneeling: A. Bond, D. Watts, R. Janaway, I. Renshaw, M. Garman, L. Slatter, W. Williams, M. Cobb, B. Brewster, W. Workman.

Bletchley teenagers in the '40s and '50s...

Right: The young Bob Berry, 1946-7.

Bottom left: 'Off to see Cliff : five young ladies from a large party of Bletchley rock'n'roll fans waiting for the coach to take them to London to see and hear Cliff Richards' (sic).
(Gazette 30.7.60)

Bottom right: This photograph shows the 1843 High Street Methodist Chapel which was converted to the County Cinema in 1911, and closed down in 1957.

There was absolutely nowhere to go courting. The outlooks were different then. My future mother-in-law said my girlfriend had to be in by 10 pm. There were two picture palaces - the County on Watling Street and the Studio in Bletchley Road. My Dad took an extremely dim view if we went to the pictures on a Sunday evening. So we used to walk up Bletchley Road to the refreshment rooms on the station, have a cup of tea and a piece of cake, and that was our Sunday night out! It used to be quite grim.

Bob Berry

We are informed that small gangs of noisy youths and girls are, by their behaviour, spoiling the enjoyment of other patrons at the local cinemas. A determined effort is being made by the managements to stop the nuisance. Most of the youths are not natives of the town. Some come in from nearby places where similar behaviour is not tolerated.

(Gazette 25.6.56)

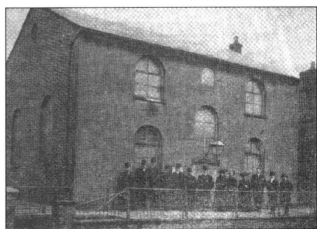

'JIVING' TO BE BANNED? Wilton Avenue residents declare they will fight 'tooth and nail' for the removal of the hall as a dance hall : jiving 'takes up too much room and trouble starts when other dancers object'; people 'tried to get in at every conceivable place, including the toilet windows'; and 'when the police have not been there, there has been trouble from those trying to get in from the outside and those urging them on from the inside' - stewards 'had to barricade themselves in.',

(Gazette 30.6.56)

Top: 'Traditional jazz' fans at Wilton Hall, 1960.

Centre: Dancing to the 'Top Pops' at Wilton Hall in 1960.

Bottom left: 'Rock'n'roll enthusiasts enjoying themselves at R.A.A.'s first rock'n'roll session at Yeomanry Hall, Bletchley.' *(Gazette 23.3.57).*

Bottom right: Bletchley jivers in 1961.

'Of many of the so-called Teddy Boys, the great majority will make very fine citizens and I think it is our duty as seniors and as Young Conservatives for the best of the Teddy Boys to be welcomed into the Young Conservative movement ...no matter how long their hair was or how tight their trousers.'

Sir Frank Markham,
quoted in the 'Gazette' 1961

Above: Teddy Boys at Wilton Hall, 1961

Right: Sir Frank Markham (centre), President of the Bletchley Operatic Society, presenting parting gifts to Mr. and Mrs. W.K. Lewis at a social evening in October, 1966.

There's a good story about the 'Greenways' cafe : there was a film about at the time where the hero puts the money in the juke-box and roars up the road and round and round, and has to get back before the juke-box stops playing. One of the local lads tried to play that out there - he's come out of the cafe and is on his motorbike, gives it some wellie, and he's looking round to watch everyone, and wallop! - he's gone right up the back of a Sunbeam Talbot, right outside the Co-op as it used to be. I don't think he broke anything, but he gave everyone a good laugh and a fright!

Barry Brace

Left: 'All ready for a burn-up...17-year old Sandra Newman, pictured with 17-year old Alan Vaughan, says : `I like the speed and to feel the wind in my hair!`' (Gazette, 1961)

Below: The Bletchley Youth Club preparing for the new season, 1962 : Barrie Field (bearded) is in the centre of the picture.

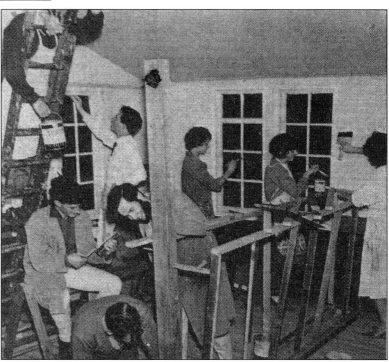

...and in the '60s...

Right: *The Animals at Wilton Hall, July, 1964.*

Centre: *The Wilton Hall advert for Spring, 1964.*

Far right: *Alan Price and Johnny Steel of The Animals*

Bottom left: *The Rolling Stones signing autographs during the interval of their performance at Wilton Hall in March, 1964.*

Bottom right: *The Hollies at Wilton Hall, November, 1964.*

At the Wilton Hall we used to have a dance a week, and back in the '60s you got most of the big bands - The Rolling Stones appeared at Bletchley, The Animals, the Searchers, the Troggs, everyone bar the Beatles.

Alan Marshall

A guy called King ran the show at Wilton Hall ; I actually booked the Rolling Stones, the Barron Knights, the Animals - I talked to Eric Burden. I got involved through the Youth Club I ran at the church when I was 17.

Barrie Field

When the Rolling Stones came down, part of the wall actually fell down at the front. I couldn't get in, and as the girls came screaming out 'cause the wall was falling down, we just walked in and the band carried on playing!

Gordon Ridgway

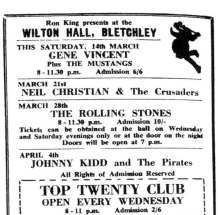

Ron King presents at the
WILTON HALL, BLETCHLEY
THIS SATURDAY, 14th MARCH
GENE VINCENT
Plus THE MUSTANGS
8 - 11.30 p.m.   Admission 6/6

MARCH 21st
NEIL CHRISTIAN & The Crusaders

MARCH 28th
THE ROLLING STONES
8 - 11.30 p.m.   Admission 10/-
Tickets can be obtained at the hall on Wednesday and Saturday evenings only or at the door on the night Doors will be open at 7 p.m.

APRIL 4th
JOHNNY KIDD and The Pirates
All Rights of Admission Reserved

TOP TWENTY CLUB
OPEN EVERY WEDNESDAY
8 - 11 p.m.   Admission 2/6

We used to walk down to the Queensway, we'd go to the record shops, the pictures, the Central Gardens and the tennis courts...and you met people from school and you just sort of roamed.

Stephen Flinn

On a Saturday, you went down to Makarios' coffee bar. You'd sit there with your mates and someone else'd come in, and the table'd get bigger and bigger - and this was across schools, because your abiding interest was music, the Beatles and all that...You'd sit there forever over one cup of coffee. It was great, with the old clear glass cups and saucers.

Stephen Flinn

Above: *The Animals.*

Centre left: *The Bletchley beat group, The Sceptres, playing at the Scott Meat company dance in April, 1966. (Left to right, Roy West, Peter Olford, Alan Brothwell and Gordon Hart).*

Bottom right: *Wilton Hall in August, 1966, with Jo Jo Gunne on stage.*

Others: *The Wilton Hall audiences 1964-6*

In 1966...

- England won the World Cup;
- Henry Cooper knocked down Cassius Clay;
- Radio Caroline broadcast illegally from the North Sea;
- Comprehensive Schools were taking over from Grammar Schools;
- The Aberfan disaster killed over 100 children;
- Iron and steel were renationalised;
- Manufacturing employment reached its peak of 8.7 million;
- Labour increased its majority at the General Election;
- Mods and Rockers fought running battles at seaside towns...

...and the Queen came to Bletchley!

Right: An extract from the official programme of the Queen's visit, 4.4.66

*Above: The Bletchley Youth Club Football Team, 1966, having just beaten Newport Pagnell Wanderers 1 - 0 at the North Bucks League Presentation Match. **Back row:** (left to right) Terry Hatton, Kevin Bowen, John Robertson, Trevor Davies and Pete Miller. **Front row:** Roger Martin, Doug Brawn, Stephen Flinn, Alan Marshall, Bob Kemsley and Tim Dickinson.*

MONDAY, 4TH APRIL 1966

VISIT TO BLETCHLEY OF HER MAJESTY THE QUEEN AND H.R.H. THE DUKE OF EDINBURGH

Residents and visitors are advised to congregate at Simpson, Aylesbury Street, Bletchley Road and at Warwick Place the principal centre of Bletchley's welcome to Her Majesty

The Royal Procession will be:-

```
Three Press Cars                                - approx.10 mins. in advance
The Lord Lieutenant's Car                       - approx. 5 mins. in advance
Warning Car (Police White Jaguar)              - 2 mins. in advance
Two Police Motor Cycles
Pilot Car (White Jaguar) with Chief Constable
```

THE ROYAL CAR

```
Car with Members of Royal Household
Police Car (White Jaguar)
Two Press Cars
Two Police Motor Cycles
```

TIMETABLE OF THE ROYAL PROCESSION

3.42 p.m.   Simpson Village - slow speed near School.
3.46 p.m.   Aylesbury Street - slow speed.
3.51 p.m.   Bletchley Road - slow speed from Leon Schools to Grammar School.
4.01 p.m.   Warwick Place - Royal Procession arrives and leaves at
4.16 p.m.   travelling via Whaddon Way, Derwent Drive, Kennet Drive to Rivers County Infants' School, Trent Road, where the Royal Visitors will inspect the School and meet representatives of the Buckinghamshire County Council.
            The Royal Procession leaves the School and proceeds via Shenley Road, Middlesex Drive, Sussex Road, Whaddon Way,
4.42 p.m.   Church Green Road, Buckingham Road and
            at the Railway Station at

THE PROGRAMME AT WARWICK PLACE

3.15 - 4.00 p.m.   The Royal Air Force Apprentices' Drum and Pipe Band (by kind permission of Air Commodore A.C. Deere, D.S.O., O.B.E., D.F.C., and under the direction of the Bandmaster, Warrant Officer F. Bailey, B.E.M.) will render selections and give a display.

4.01 - 4.16 p.m.   Her Majesty The Queen and H.R.H. The Duke of Edinburgh will be heralded on arrival by a cohort of the Band's Trumpeters and received by the Lord Lieutenant, Brigadier Sir Henry Floyd, Bt., C.B., C.B.E.

The Lord Lieutenant will present the Chairman of the Council (Councillor J.F. Cassidy, J.P.), Mrs. Cassidy and the Clerk of the Council.

Other presentations will follow.

The Royal Visitors will be invited to sign the Distinguished Visitors' Book and then to visit the nearby house, No.72 Warwick Road.

The departure of the Royal Party will be accompanied by a further fanfare from the Trumpeters.

THE CHAIRMAN AND MEMBERS OF THE BLETCHLEY URBAN DISTRICT COUNCIL INVITE YOU TO HELP BLETCHLEY GIVE A RIGHT ROYAL WELCOME TO HER MAJESTY AND HIS ROYAL HIGHNESS.

[IV] The Queen's Visit...

Left: 'The Spence family of 72 Warwick Place, who were chosen to have the Queen and Prince Philip as visitors on April 4th : Mr. and Mrs. W.J.F. Spence with sons Colin and Neil (right)' - Gazette 11.3.66.

Above: 'A delightful picture of the Queen just after leaving the home of Mr. and Mrs. W. Spence' (Cllr. Jim Cassidy is behind her - Gazette, 7.4.66).

...the officers' view :

They erected quite extensive staging on that Warwick Road open space...Immediately on the Queen arriving, she was met by myself accompanying the chief citizen of the district - the chairman of the council, Jim Cassidy, who presented the people on the platform - the council, and the heads of chief organisations. I understand John Smithie was speaking about how Bletchley had grown and was still expanding. I understand Prince Phillip asked, 'Why do you want it to be so big?' I don't know what the answer was.

Harold Hudson

Above: The Queen with the Boys' Brigade in the foreground. Arthur Grigg is in the background, representing the NUR - 'the largest and most active Trade Union in the new Bletchley' (Arthur Grigg).

Below: 'Part of the crowd which fronted the presentation dais. The Queen is just going towards the Spence's house while the Duke (partly hidden by a pillar) lingers behind.' (Gazette, 7.4.66)

We'd been trying, on the Council, to get rid of this silly 'Bletchley Road, Bletchley' idea. All the traders said, 'No, no. Cost us money to reprint our noteheads' and so on. Then the Queen came...We had a meeting of the Labour group and the Chairman said, 'How can we commemorate the Queen's visit, because we can't spend a lot of money, we can't afford it.' I had a brainwave and said, 'Look, we'll change the name of Bletchley Road to Queensway, because she travelled up there.' They jumped at it and said, 'Well, nobody will dare oppose that.' And they didn't!

Ron Staniford

Newport Pagnell Urban (District Council) presented the Queen with a bouquet, but we were better : we went down to Ramsbothams and one of the assistants made the suggestion, 'Let's make a nice posy of freesias. The Queen likes them. I've seen any number of photographs when she was carrying a bunch of freesias.'

I said, 'Right.' All the bouquets had been handed over to the Ladies-in-waiting, but she was still carrying that bunch of freesias when she got on the train at Bletchley Station at the end of the visit.

Harold Hudson

Above: Presentation to the Queen of the Councillors in the marquee at Warwick Place. Left to right : Cllr. Jim Cassidy (Chairman of Bletchley Urban District Council); the Queen; Ted Edwards; Bruce Hardwick; Cecil Bowden; Frank Bowman; Jack White; Tom Dickens; Fred Parkin; John Smithie.

Left: 'A bouquet for the Queen from Mrs. J Cassidy. Cllr J. Cassidy looks on, but the Duke seems interested elsewhere.' (Gazette, 7.4.66).

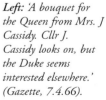

...the people's view :

I was one of the Girl Guides who lined the route. What a day that was! It was unbelievable. I had to stand up straight in full uniform. Who would have thought the Queen would have come to Bletchley? She went into this house : it was all decorated up.

Gisella Perry

Right: Scouts crowd to get a view of the Queen as she leaves the Spence's home.

Below: Children in Aylesbury Street.

Bottom: The Royal Car, cheered by children from Leon Schools.

I was working at Castles School at the time, and all the children had little flags to wave and we made posters, 'God save the Queen' and all these sorts of things. She came past the school. All the children had been very excited about it. It was a lovely day, and she and the Duke of Edinburgh came up in this wonderful car. She really did look lovely. I think she was quite an attractive woman really, looked better in the flesh. So she got out and walked up to this house. Everybody waved their flags and the whole incident was over in about 10 minutes and it was a bit of an anti-climax. Anyhow, it was exciting.

Betty Watts

If you get on the Buckingham Road...up on the right hand side where the new houses were built - she had tea in there. It was a big thing because Sylvie took the kids up there. There was loads of people as you can imagine.

Frank Bodimeade

I went down the station - on that corner - that's where I saw her just come out.

Betty Clifford

I took the girls down - the youngest one was in the pushchair and the other one was walking. We went down the street opposite the Post Office to see the Queen...I think she'd got a nice green costume ... it was a shame really, because you were lined up on both sides - they didn't slow up that much.

Eileen Corden

I remember standing on the balcony of the cinema to watch her go by. And I thought how tiny she looked in the car. Flags - it was packed. We had a lovely view because we were up there.

Pat Flinn

Above: *Some of the youngest spectators.*

Left: *Part of the 5,000 crowd at Warwick Road.*

It was absolutely cracking - everybody turned out to go and see them ... my husband should have been at work, but he wasn't 'cause he was out there filming her visit. There was lots of men. You know they packed their jobs in for perhaps half an hour, all standing there waving and cheering. She got a good reception. It was a new place, and perhaps she wanted to make it that much more popular. Once the Queen's gone there, it must be all right.

Doreen Brace

I saw her outside the school. She was lovely - her skin was perfect, beautiful. It was magic...

Iris Witcomb

Epilogue

I n 1964, the first moves had been initiated to designate an area including Bletchley, but not centred on it, as the New City of Milton Keynes. The plans both of the Buckinghamshire County Council ('Pooleyville'), and of the Bletchley Urban District Council, were dropped..

Initial enthusiasm -

The call for a Bigger, Brighter, Better Bletchley, made by the *'Gazette'* in its first issue 30 years ago, came a long step nearer to being realised on Monday when a bold and brilliant outline scheme for making a town of 150,000 people in 25 years was presented to the public by Bletchley Council.

(Gazette 5.9.64)

- gave way to consternation -

The area of the new city on virgin soil which the Bucks County Planning Committee thinks should be built...is exactly what Bletchley feared : it would be straddled by a 250,000-souled colossus...with the village of Loughton at the centre.

(Gazette 21.11.64)

- and frustration :

1964, Bletchley's year of great expectations has ended as Bletchley's year of frustrations. Leap year it was, but not for the town's further anticipated expansion. There were plans and counter-plans, but the go-ahead for the development...never came. The New Year opens in indecision, with some non-committal promises that Bletchley will be all right, but with the mushroom-cloud of the pipe-dream city - 'Pooleyville', 'Whaddon', 'Loughton', 'Chiltern', call it what you will - hanging over town and area. We live in a funny age if, as would seem to be the case, the lusty town, anxious to grow, is neglected in favour of an embryo city so recently conceived and destined for a long period of gestation, if ever it is born...Bletchley's own big-town plan, like the County plan, will never come to pass.

(Gazette 2.1.65)

Below left: Bletchley Council delegates on their way to meet the Ministry to discuss North Bucks development : Cllr. F. Evans, Mr. J.F. Smithie (Surveyor), Mr. N. Chambers (Treasurer), Mr. H.V. Hudson (Clerk), Cllr. C. Head, Cllr. J. Cassidy, Cllr. W. Caldwell.'
(Gazette 5.6.64)

Below right: The meeting in Wilton Hall to launch the 150,000 population plan, September, 1964. Len May and Robert Maxwell are in the front row.

Bletchley needed a new direction...

'None of us can be proud of Bletchley as it is now,' Cllr. J. Cassidy told Fenny Stratford parishioners last week. The planned expansion had created to some extent a one-class town...but now the wonderful educational opportunities for youngsters had created a need for more than factory jobs. 'We need to encourage technical, electronic, computer and service industries.' If expansion did not come, then the only thing they would have created was a place for some people to come and live in until the children grew up.

(Gazette 19.11.65)

...and the new city of Milton Keynes was to provide it

STOP PRESS - New City Study : An 86-page report published today favours new city expansion to the north of Bletchley...

(Gazette 3.12.65)

The outline plan for Milton Keynes.

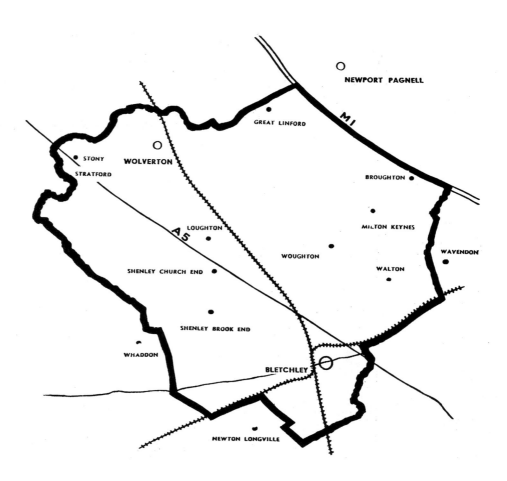

As for the original 'settlers'...

I never think I go back... it's all here, you know. I very happy now, you know, because I got my own house. My *familia* are very close to me, you know. Never mind in Italy beautiful house, but I like this place. I enjoy myself. I live happy life.

Giovanni Palmiero

We've got six grandchildren, it's lovely really. So our roots are in Bletchley. We said if we ever won the Lottery, we wouldn't want to move out of Bletchley, no never move. We moved out once and see our mistake and come back. Never move again, not out of Bletchley.

Alec Clifford

Above: The Palmiero family. Giovanni and Serafina are on the right of the picture with Sabrina in front of them. Next to her, Sophie, then Bradley, Carlo and Giancarlo. Behind them, Maria holding Angelica.

Left: The Clifford family. Alec and Betty Clifford with their six grandchildren: (left to right) Lewis, Kerry, Tom and Amy Clifford, and in front, Emily and Polly Smith.

Both photos taken in October 1996.

Acknowledgements

Contributors : the personal memories, photographs, first-hand accounts, and verbatim interview extracts in this book are a marvellous example of the rich vein of historical sources running through a local community. Many thanks to : *Dick Arnold; Vera Barrow; Bob Berry; Bill and Joan Burchell; Frank Bodimeade; Barry, Doreen and Michael Brace; Meg Bates; Bobby and Mrs. Bunn; Wendy Checkley; Marjorie Clarke; Alec and Betty Clifford; Eileen Corden; Roland Doggett; Rosemary Evans; Barrie and Ted Field; Patricia, Ronald and Stephen Flinn; Arthur Grigg; Bruce Hardwick; Harold Hudson; Ted Legg; Alan and Wendy Marshall; Jim Marshall; Roy Maycock; Winifred Ottery; Laura Owen; Pietro, Giovanni and Serafina Palmiero; Gisella Perry; Mr. and Mrs. Ernest Perkins; Pam Porter; Mrs. Rashdi; Gordon and Linda Ridgway; Anne Sanders; John Smithie; Irene Spanner; Ron Staniford; Betty Watts; Iris Witcomb; members of the Bletchley Mothers' Club, especially Monica Austin, Brenda Monaghan, Daphne Taylor and 'Margaret'; and members of the Bletchley 'Toc H'.*

Interviewers : The Living Archive Project mobilises a huge army of volunteers in its many community arts ventures. For this one, many thanks to the interviewing expertise of : *Michael Brace, Robert Excell, Stephen Flinn, Jenny Freeman, Roger Kitchen, Sheila Lindsay, Claire Newton, David Newton, Kay Peck, Sue Quinn, and Jane Turner.*

Newspaper sources : The negatives of photographs used from the erstwhile 'Bletchley and District Gazette' have disappeared in spite of our exhaustive searches to trace them. Therefore, the considerable help given by the *Milton Keynes Museum of Industry and Rural Life* (especially Bill Griffiths) and the advice, support and permission given by the *Milton Keynes Citizen* (especially Steve Larner and Nick Hammond) are much appreciated.

Design : Many thanks for the expertise, talents and patient professionalism of *Dylan Jeavons.*

Other sources : The photograph of Whaddon Way by Francis Swift on Page 15 is used with permission from Julian Hunt of the *Aylesbury County Reference Library.* Thanks to Denis Gurney and other sources for photographs of Bletchley market on page 19. Thanks also to *Milton Keynes Borough Council and Southern Arts Board* whose continued financial support makes Living Archive projects like this possible.

Finally, my personal thanks to colleagues at *Living Archive Project* - Herbert Booth, Rob Hunt, Dave Rogerson, and particularly, Zena Flinn and Sue Quinn; and a special thanks to *LAP's* General Manager, Roger Kitchen : as co-author with Rib Davis of the related drama-documentary, Bigger, Brighter, Better! (performed 5th - 12th December, 1996, at The Sanctuary, Bletchley), Roger inspired both the structure of this book and many avenues of research. For a 'first-timer', this was invaluable.

Marion Hill

Below: Aerial picture of Bletchley, 1962.

Bottom: Extract from the 'Gazette', 1962.

INDUSTRIAL BLETCHLEY

LOOKING SOUTH TOWARDS LONDON (above GG2206), showing, at the top in the "V" formed by the Watling Street and the Bedford branch line, the Terrapin Ltd. factory, J. Telley and Co. Ltd. (with the "saw-tooth" roofing) and W. O. Peake Ltd. (with the Rodexians' cricket field behind). On the other side of the railway line at this point can

ten the print works of Claridge Lewis & Jordan (Bletchley) Ltd., opposite Mr. Charles Head's works and Mr. Deighton's nurseries, and further to the right, Hills & Richard's carpet factory, and the new bus depot. ing back to the industrial estate itself, MacLean Bros. (Paper) Ltd. and the flat-roofed works of M. F. Robertshaw Ltd. are opposite the service-road entrance. Behind are the railway sidings (including to the right, ew rail electrification depot) and with the railway cottages (now demolished) at the foot of the embankment. Next to Robertshaw's is Berry's Electric Magicoal Ltd. (with the square windows in the roof) and just te First Avenue is Ellisdon's, with the temporary buildings for County Furniture behind, and further along, G. W. Every & Sons Ltd. First Avenue itself has now been extended and brought round to join Third Avenue, opening up the vacant land on the right to provide the town's "No. 3 estate." The five-bay factory with considerable open frontage to the service-road is Dyson & Co., Enfield (1919) Ltd. Next fronting the service- is Associated British Paper Patterns Ltd., with Filtrona Developments Ltd. behind and fronting Second Avenue, followed by Scot Meat Products (soon to have a much larger place on No. 3 estate) and Foundry nisations (Baillot) Ltd. The factory with the car park in front is High Precision Equipment Ltd., and at the bottom of the picture, with the curved driveways are the former Wipac Group factories, now owned by the Council. On the left-hand side of the Watling Street just beyond the service road entrance is Beacon Brushes Ltd., and the building in the top left-hand corner is the new county highways' depot.